T is for Teachers

A School Alphabet

Written by Steven L. Layne and Deborah Dover Layne
Illustrated by Doris Ettlinger

Sleeping Bear Press™
310 North Main Street, Suite 300
Chelsea, MI 48118
www.sleepingbearpress.com

© 2005 Thomson Gale, a part of the Thomson Corporation.

Thomson, Star Logo and Sleeping Bear Press are trademarks
and Gale is a registered trademark used herein under license.

Printed and bound in Canada.

10 9 8 7 6 5 4 3 2 1 (pbk)
10 9 8 7 6 5 4 3 (case)

Library of Congress Cataloging-in-Publication Data

Layne, Steven L.
T is for teachers : a school alphabet / by Steven L. Layne and
Deborah Dover Layne ; illustrated by Doris Ettlinger.
p. cm.
Summary: "An A-Z pictorial for children ages 4-10 explaining school. Letter
topics include, the alphabet, kindergarten, books, librarian, and principal.
Each is introduced with a poem accompanied by expository text to provide
detailed information"—Provided by publisher.

pbk   ISBN13: 978-1-58536-331-5   case ISBN 13: 978-1-58536-159-5
      ISBN 10: 1-58536-331-6   ISBN 10: 1-58536-159-3

1. Schools—Juvenile literature. 2. Alphabet books—Juvenile literature.
 I. Layne, Deborah Dover. II. Ettlinger, Doris, ill. III. Title.
LB1556.L39 2005
371—dc22   2004027301

To Carol Crane, who teaches so much to so many...and always with great love.
Thanks for being in my corner.

STEVE

For two of my favorite aunts, Sue Roberts and Sue Groves—
great educators who fostered a love of teaching in me from my earliest years.

DEBBIE

To the teachers of Port Colden and Brass Castle Schools.

DORIS

Inside every schoolhouse
there's much to do and see.
Let's look at all that makes school fun;
we'll work from **A** to **Z**.

"Writing" first appeared as sketches drawn on walls of caves. As time passed, advanced ways of communicating emerged. First pictures of words and ideas appeared. Then came pictures of syllables, and finally, an alphabet. An alphabet is made up of symbols for the sounds we use in speaking. This process took thousands of years and the talents and imaginations of lots of people. The English alphabet can be traced back in history to the Roman alphabet, which can be traced back to the ancient script of the Phoenicians. People borrowed from each other and shared ideas over time to create the alphabet that exists today.

The alphabet consists of 26 letters. In school these letters are written in both manuscript (printing) and cursive styles of writing. Students also learn the difference between using uppercase, or capital letters, and lowercase, or small letters. One common way teachers help students learn the letters of the alphabet is by singing the alphabet song.

A begins our Alphabet—
the letters that we need
to make the words and sentences
we want to write and read.

Bb

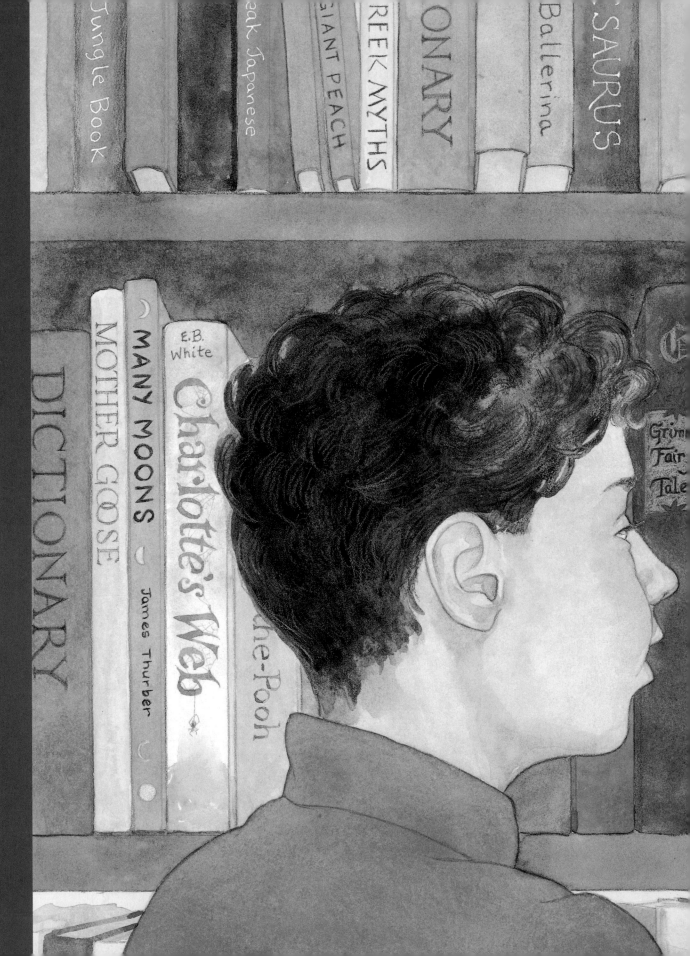

Teachers use many different kinds of books to help students learn. One special book is called a teacher's manual. It helps instructors plan what to teach in each subject area. Some other examples of books students will find in school include picture books, chapter books, young adult novels, biographies (books about famous people written by someone else), autobiographies (books about famous people written by the person himself), encyclopedias, dictionaries, and the thesaurus. Students also use textbooks in many of their classes. Examples of textbooks include spelling books, math books, science books, and workbooks. Most books fall into one of two categories—fiction or nonfiction. Books classified as fiction are stories that are not true and are made up in the author's imagination. Books classified as nonfiction are books that give factual or true information about a certain topic.

What fills many shelves in school?
They start with letter **B**.
Of course, they're Books
that tell us about facts and fantasy.

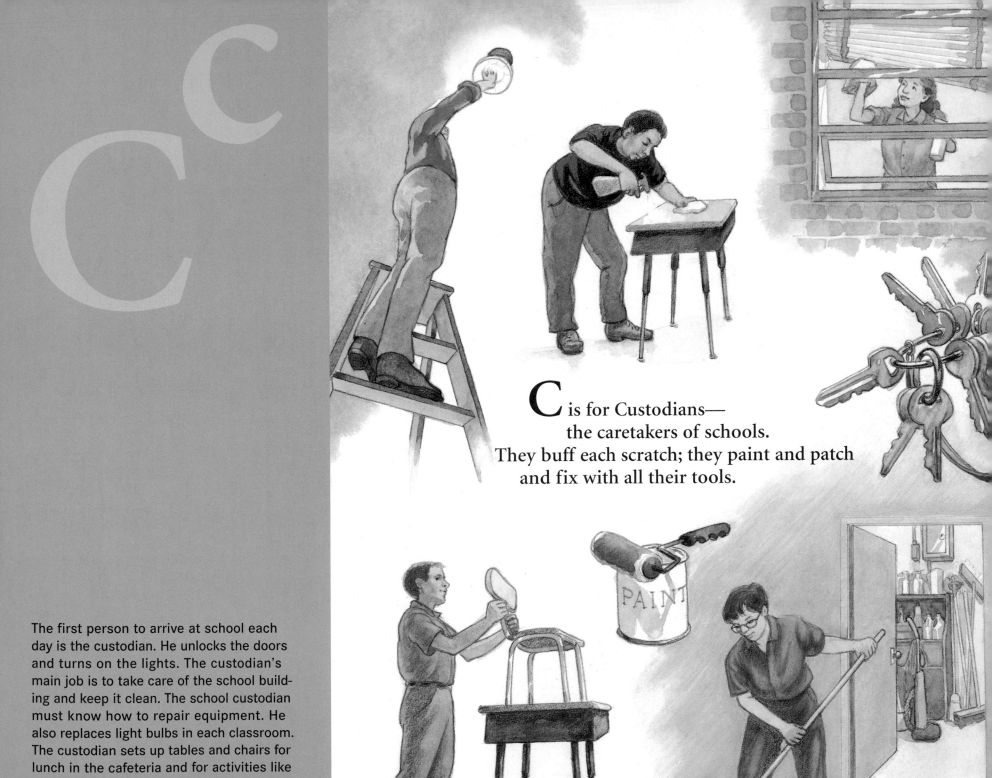

C is for Custodians—
the caretakers of schools.
They buff each scratch; they paint and patch
and fix with all their tools.

The first person to arrive at school each day is the custodian. He unlocks the doors and turns on the lights. The custodian's main job is to take care of the school building and keep it clean. The school custodian must know how to repair equipment. He also replaces light bulbs in each classroom. The custodian sets up tables and chairs for lunch in the cafeteria and for activities like concerts, meetings, and sporting events. It is the custodian's job to keep track of the materials needed to keep the school clean and to manage the unloading of delivery trucks and the distribution of orders and supplies. He also vacuums, empties garbage cans, and makes sure the school building is clean and safe for the next school day.

A dictionary is a special book. It contains all of the words we use to speak and write. Next to each entry word is a set of parentheses containing each word's pronunciation. Then an abbreviation is given that tells what part of speech each word can be used as, and finally the definition is given. A definition is an explanation of what each word means. Sometimes words can have more than one meaning. In this case, each definition is numbered.

In the primary grades it is common to find students using picture dictionaries. These dictionaries usually contain short and simple definitions along with a picture to help students better understand word meanings.

D d

The Dictionary holds our words.
It starts with letter D.
Inside are definitions
and a pronunciation key.

Our **E** is Education—
the goal of school each day
to foster a desire to learn
that never goes away.

The most common way to gain knowledge and skill is by going to school to receive an education. In both the United States and Canada, public school is free for all students and is offered from kindergarten through 12th grade. Learning about math, science, social studies, reading, writing, art, music, and physical education is what school is all about. After high school graduation, students can make the choice to continue their education by going to college or a vocational school where specific job or career training takes place. Having a good education is especially helpful to students later in life when they are ready to choose a career.

Some families choose to teach their children at home (home-schooling) instead of sending them to a school building. In this type of education Mom or Dad is usually the teacher, and the children work at their own pace in each subject area.

A third type of education takes place in what are called private schools. Some private schools specialize in specific academic areas like math or science or are associated with a specific religious group. Anywhere learning takes place helps provide an education. For example, a family vacation can provide the opportunity for a lot of excellent learning.

our **F**, the Flag, *Old Glory*.
She flies unfurled—
a symbol of our mighty nation's story.

Flags have powerful meaning. This flag stands for the United States of America. The flag's red, white, and blue colors and its stars and stripes represent the American spirit. Red stands for courage and bravery. White stands for purity and innocence, and blue stands for truth and loyalty. The 50 stars represent each state, and the 13 stripes represent the original 13 colonies that fought to separate from Great Britain and form a new country—America. Other names for our flag include *Old Glory*; *Stars and Stripes*; *the Red, White, and Blue*; and *the Star-Spangled Banner*.

Each school day, millions of students in classrooms across America stand with their hands over their hearts and recite the Pledge of Allegiance to our nation's flag. The pledge is a promise of loyalty to our country. Francis Bellamy wrote the pledge in 1892.

Ff

Gymnasium begins with **G**.
We show up there to have P.E.,
a class that keeps us toned and trim
and teaches us to lose and win.

Physical education is a special subject. It is also called gym class or P.E. Gym class is a favorite part of the school day for many students because they get a chance to be active and loud. The gym teacher is a coach and guide who demonstrates basic skills for playing games such as soccer, basketball, baseball, volleyball, and individual activities like gymnastics and swimming. Helping students learn how to stay fit is an important part of the job. This is accomplished by teaching students about proper eating habits and exercise. Gym teachers are proud of their students' accomplishments and help them learn to be graceful winners and losers who show good sportsmanship.

In elementary school the study of history takes place in a class called social studies. During the primary grades students learn about their neighborhoods and communities as well as special holidays with ties to history.

Some of the topics covered in the intermediate grades include early explorers, Indians, and the Pilgrims. Near the Thanksgiving holiday students study the Pilgrims, their journey across the ocean to the New World, and how they broke away from England to establish a new country— the United States of America. To help students understand Pilgrim life, many teachers try to recreate this time in history by having students participate in a special Thanksgiving feast like the one the Pilgrims shared.

The history of the Revolutionary War, how our government was formed, and the celebration of the 4th of July are all important events in our country's history. Students in the upper elementary grades enjoy learning about these topics as well as studying information about ancient civilizations and world history.

H
h

H stands for History.
These stories from the past
are studied in our schools each year
so memories will last.

In art class students learn to paint and illustrate. An illustration can be a drawing. Art teachers help their students understand that artists tell stories and communicate ideas and feelings through pictures. The materials an artist uses are called "media." Media refers to the materials used to create a piece of art. Some examples of media include chalk, paint, crayons, and clay. Media is different than the tools that an artist uses to assist in creating art. An artist's tools might include things like brushes, rollers, trays, scissors, or pliers.

Some famous artists students learn about in school include Michelangelo, Pablo Picasso, Leonardo Da Vinci, Georgia O'Keeffe, and Walt Disney. Students also learn some of the elements artists work with including line, shape, texture, form, space, value, and color. Two important color families are the primary colors and secondary colors. The primary colors are red, yellow, and blue. Mixing any two of the primary colors together will result in the secondary colors which are purple, orange, and green.

Ii

Illustration is a skill.
In art class you'll learn why
this talent gives our eyes a treat
and starts with letter I.

In science class we find our J—
a planet that is far away.
It's Jupiter—this planet's got
a giant storm, the Great Red Spot!

One of the many topics covered in elementary science class is the solar system. Our solar system has eight planets and a sun. These planets include Earth, Mars, Venus, Jupiter, Saturn, Neptune, Mercury, and Uranus. Pluto was our ninth planet until August 2006 when a group of scientists downgraded Pluto from an official planet to a dwarf planet. Many students love science class because of the hands-on nature of learning. Doing experiments is a lot of fun as students see, hear, touch, smell, and feel while learning about the world around them.

Jj

Students learn the letters of the alphabet and their sounds in kindergarten. Learning how to take turns, raise your hand, follow directions, and clean up are also important tasks that are new for many kindergarten students. They also spend time learning how to work and share together, practicing their numbers, and counting to at least 100! Some children even begin to write simple words and sentences and to read easy books by the end of kindergarten. The word "kindergarten" comes from a German word that means "a garden of children."

Kindergarten was started in the United States in 1856 by German-born Margarethe Meyer Schurz who had been a teacher in the United Kingdom. While living in Wisconsin she taught her daughter and other young children, and thus kindergarten began.

Our first school year begins with K—
a classroom where we find each day
is full of learning, friends, and fun.
Yes, Kindergarten's number one.

The person in charge of the school library is the librarian; sometimes she is called the media specialist. Ordering and organizing all of the books and materials in the library each school year is her responsibility. Sometimes she gives book talks to help students and teachers learn about new books and authors. She also reads aloud to help promote excitement for reading. The school librarian reads many books herself and can then help students find books they will enjoy reading. Librarians also teach students about research skills so they can find and use information.

Many libraries have computers. Sometimes librarians help students and teachers use different computer programs. Because the library is such a busy center for student learning, it is important to remember to be quiet while in the library so that everyone can concentrate. The librarian enjoys sharing her love of reading with the entire school community!

Librarians—a super L.
In "matchmaking" they're leading.
They find great books for everyone
and keep the whole school reading!

M is for Mathematics class.
It's like a chest of loot.
Inside we learn to problem solve,
to reason and compute.

The operations of addition, subtraction, multiplication, and division known as arithmetic come from the Greek word *arithmos*, which means "number." Students can compute or find the answer to a math problem by using these four operations. However, in math class students learn more than just computation skills. Teachers know it is also important for their students to learn reasoning and problem solving skills. These skills are necessary for dealing with ordinary, everyday activities such as grocery shopping and balancing a checkbook.

M m

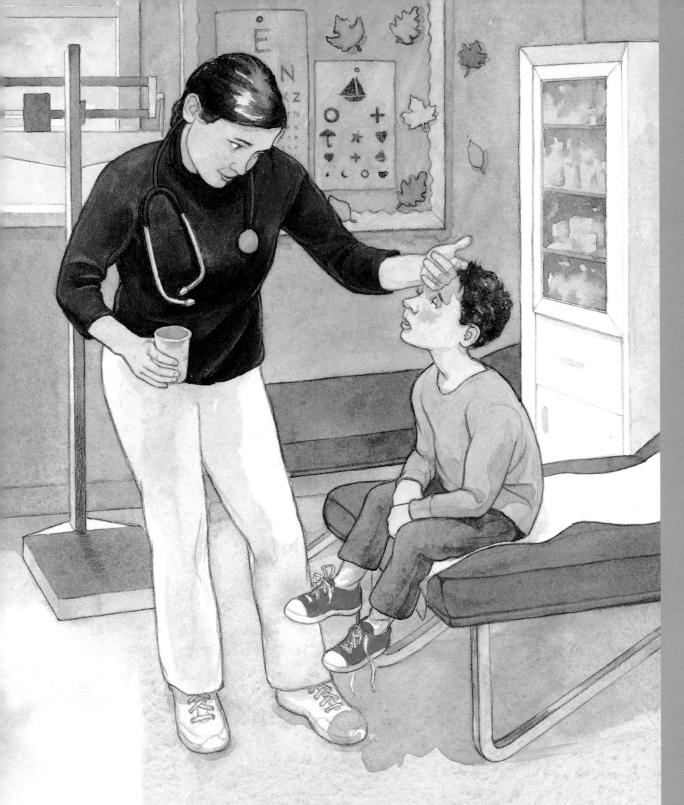

When we aren't well and need some care
there's someone who is always there.
This **N** who hears of every ache
is our school Nurse—make no mistake!

The school nurse helps students who are not feeling well. She might take a child's temperature or decide if it is necessary for the student to go home. If an emergency happens during the school day, the nurse knows how to contact the family doctor if necessary. With a parent's permission, the school nurse also gives medicine to students during the school day. Another important responsibility the school nurse has is reviewing student records to make sure all of the medical information is up-to-date.

From the 1700s to the 1950s more than seven generations of children attended one-room schools. Some famous people who were educated here include Presidents Washington and Lincoln and Laura Ingalls Wilder. Inside the classroom, girls sat on one side of the room and boys on the other. Students ranged in age from 4 to 18 years old, and there were usually no more than 30 students attending each school. Students originally studied reading, writing, arithmetic, and religion. Over the years spelling, penmanship, grammar, history, geography, literature, and Latin were added. Older students assisted the teacher by tutoring the younger children. Students were grouped according to their ability and progress. The one-room school was the center of the community, a symbol of a shared community life. Currently, in the United States, there are still a few one-room schoolhouses in existence.

Many grades of school
were taught together long ago
inside a One-room schoolhouse
which becomes our letter O.

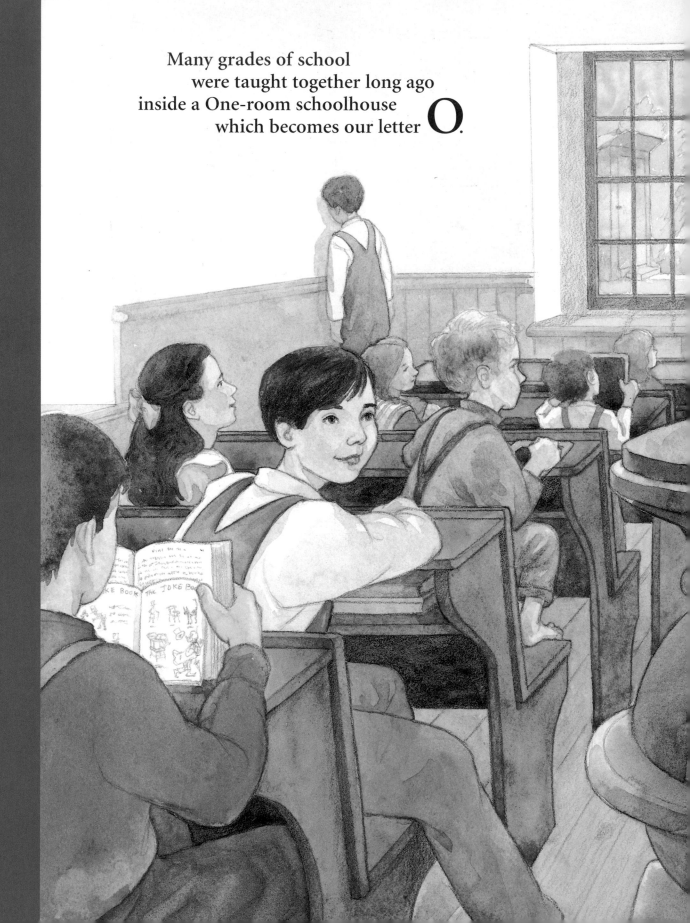

A principal's most important job is to be the leader of the school. Every day school principals make important decisions. They hire teachers. They also visit classrooms and help teachers plan strong lessons. Principals study test scores in order to find better ways for students to learn. Principals talk with students, parents, teachers, and the community. School principals care about students and teachers and encourage them to do their best work. Principals work with parents and teachers to create the best learning environment for students. They share information about what students are doing with the community and seek to form partnerships with community members and the school. Principals help establish and enforce rules in order to keep students safe.

Which people in our school buildings will lead us all year long?
None other than our Principals—
the **P**s that make schools strong.

A quiz is different than a test. Usually a quiz is shorter, is given more frequently, and covers less information than a test. Taking a quiz gives children a chance to show how much they have learned. The scores from a quiz also help the teacher know who is ready to study new things and who needs more time to learn the current information.

Quizzes are short tests
that don't take long for us to do.
They show the teachers what's been learned
and start with letter Q.

The skills and love of Reading
can take us near and far.
Just think of all the fun we'll have
because of letter R.

Learning to read is one of the most important skills students learn in elementary school. Some of the earliest signs that students are beginning to read happen when they recognize things like their own name, traffic signs like a stop sign, or the name of their favorite cereal on a box in the grocery store. Another way students demonstrate beginning reading is by memorizing easy picture book stories and reading them either from memory or by using picture clues. Being able to read helps students become successful in many other areas of school as well, and in life outside of school. Just as important as learning how to read is having a desire to read and a love of reading. Teachers work hard to help children love reading by sharing great stories with them. Many teachers share these stories by reading them out loud to their students each day and by providing a set time each day for students to read silently on their own.

R r

The glue that holds a school together
starts with letter S.
They're Secretaries, and their work
makes staff and kids feel blessed.

S s

The school secretary is responsible for helping everyone! Parents, students, teachers, principals, visitors, and the community depend on her for assistance and important information. The secretary answers the telephone and takes messages. She also types letters, schedules, and reports for the principal. Every day she goes through the mail and delivers it to the correct mailboxes. The school secretary keeps track of student attendance. When visitors come to the school, she provides directions and answers many questions. Secretaries also use the intercom system to make announcements for the entire school and to contact individual classrooms with important messages. Everyone in the school community relies on the secretary to make each day a success.

Teachers are very special people. They care about children and want to help them learn new things. Teachers try to make learning fun and interesting by using many different kinds of materials. Pictures, games, charts, maps, computers, books, videos, demonstrations, and field trips are some of the learning tools teachers use. They are patient, encouraging, and never give up. If one teaching method doesn't work, good teachers will try another method until their students meet with success. The teachers' day doesn't end when school is over. They still have lots of work to do. Grading papers, attending meetings and parent conferences, planning future lessons, and supervising extracurricular school activities are all important tasks teachers need to do after school hours. Teaching is hard work but being able to make a difference in the lives of children and helping them learn successfully is what makes teachers happy.

Tt

T is for Teachers,
forever sowing seeds.
Their hope and prayer will always be
that every child succeeds.

Students who walk to school will find helpers along the way. Crossing guards stand on busy street corners to help keep children safe. They wear bright colored vests and on some days use umbrellas to keep children safe from the rain. Some also carry stop signs. Each time a car comes down the street, the crossing guard will signal for the car to stop and then will walk students across the street. Some crossing guards are adults, but others, usually called *safety patrols*, are older children from each elementary school who also work to help students get to school and back home again safely.

U is for Umbrellas
    that shield us from the rains.
They're held for us by crossing guards
        whose service never wanes.

Uu

V stands for Vowels.
Their friends are consonants.
They have to work together
so the words we read make sense.

There are six vowels in our language system. They include the following letters: a, e, i, o, u, and sometimes y. Vowel sounds come in two forms—long and short. Long vowels say their names like the letter a in the word "cake." The vowel y makes two different sounds. It can sound like the letter e as in the word "baby," or like the letter i as in the word "fly." Consonants are the rest of the letters in our alphabet. Consonants cannot be used alone to make words. They need the help of their vowel friends to make the words we learn to read.

Writing is an important way to communicate with others. Some of the simplest types of writing can include making a grocery list or writing a name. Several types are taught in schools including creative, narrative, persuasive, expository, and descriptive writing.

Students must also learn about the writing process. It begins with a rough draft, which is the first attempt at a writing piece. Next, students must go through the editing process, looking for mistakes that need correcting or ideas that need changing. It is helpful to have other students or teachers edit each writing piece. Then, the piece must be revised or rewritten. A writing piece can be edited and revised several times before it reaches the final stage—called publishing. It is very exciting for students to see their work in published form. Publishing can range from having the writing piece displayed on a classroom bulletin board to having it published in the school newspaper, a magazine, city newspaper, or journal.

Writing starts with **W**
and it's a skill we need
for clarity and fluid thoughts
that others, then, can read.

In music class students learn how to keep the beat. To do this, the music teacher has students use a variety of instruments including the drums, triangle, tambourine, and the xylophone. Students learn to recognize and play many different rhythms.

Another important part of music class is learning to sing by matching pitch or the tones one hears. This is usually done by learning to hear the individual notes played on a piano and then copying that note with the student's voice. Students get the opportunity to show what they have learned in music class throughout the school year by performing in school concerts, assemblies, and musicals. They might perform by singing or playing a musical instrument either as part of a group or on their own as a soloist.

In music class we'll find our X
by matching notes and tones
with voices and some instruments
like drums and Xylophones.

Y can be for Yellow.
The color of a bus
that drives from home to school and back
and takes good care of us.

The school bus is important for many students. It takes them to school and home again. Many teachers plan special field trips during the school year, and they rely on a school bus to transport all of their students to places like museums, theaters, apple orchards, pumpkin farms, and the zoo. Most school buses are yellow in color. Did you know that the law says that every time a school bus comes to a railroad crossing it must stop, open the door, and listen for the possibility of an oncoming train? The bus driver must follow many important rules in order to keep all students safe while riding a school bus.

There are also several safety rules students need to follow while riding or walking near a school bus. Students should always remain seated and listen carefully to the driver's instructions. While crossing the street in front of a school bus, students should always watch for the driver's signal, look both ways, and keep their eyes on other cars. Students should never cross in back of a school bus or reach underneath the bus.

Many teachers take their students on exciting trips. Field trips to the zoo are very popular in any grade. At the zoo, students can see all kinds of animals up close. They can also feed some of the animals. Sometimes specially trained guides called *docents* will provide new and interesting information for students as well as answer their many questions. Teachers know that the hands-on and personal experience of a field trip to the zoo is an interesting, different, and fun way for their students to learn about the many animals that inhabit our planet.

Field trips to the Zoo
are as fun as they can be.
We'll wave at bears and stare at snakes.
A perfect end—it's letter Z.

Z z

A School of Facts

1. Who is the leader of each school?

2. How many vowels are in our language system?

3. Where can you find a pronunciation key?

4. What is a short test called?

5. In which class do students learn to match notes and tones?

6. In art, what are the primary colors?

7. Where were many grades taught together long ago?

8. Name the person who keeps track of each student's attendance.

9. Who keeps students safe as they cross the streets to get to school?

10. In which class will a student work specifically with numbers?

11. What do the stars on our flag represent?

12. Who paints, cleans, and repairs our school?

13. In what class do we learn about stories from the past?

14. Name a form (type) of writing taught in elementary school.

15. Who matches students with good books to read?

16. What is the American flag sometimes called?

17. What system can we trace back to the Romans?

18. Most books fall into one of two categories. What are the names of those two categories?

Reference List

Armbruster, A. (1991). The American flag. New York, NY: Franklin Watts.

Bauld, J. S. (2000). We need principals. Mankato, MN: Pebble Books.

Beckman, B. (1985). I can be a teacher. Chicago, IL: Children's Press.

Bial, R. (1999). One-room school. Boston, MA: Houghton Mifflin Company.

Boraas, T. (1999). Community helpers: School principals. Mankato, MN: Bridgestone Books.

Burns, P. (1995). Stepping through history: Writing. New York, NY: Thomson Learning.

Deedrick, T. (1998). Community helpers: Teachers. Mankato, MN: Bridgestone Books.

Dugan, W. (1972). How our alphabet grew. New York, NY: Western Publishing Company, Inc.

Fradin, D. B. (1988). A new true book: The flag of the United States. Chicago, IL: Children's Press.

Ganeri, A. (1996). Signs of the times: The story of numbers and counting. New York, NY: Oxford University Press.

Green, C. (1998). At the school. Eden Prairie, MN: The Child's World, Inc.

Green, C. (1998). Teachers help us learn. Eden Prairie, MN: The Child's World, Inc.

Green, C. (1999). Librarians help us find information. Eden Prairie, MN: The Child's World, Inc.

Johnson, J. (1987). Community helpers series: Teachers A to Z. New York, NY: Walker & Company.

Klingel, C., and Noyed, R. B. (2001). My school helpers: School custodians. Vero Beach, FL: The Rourke Press, Inc.

Klingel, C., and Noyed, R. B. (2001). My school helpers: School media specialists. Vero Beach, FL: The Rourke Press, Inc.

Klingel, C., and Noyed, R. B. (2001). My school helpers: School secretaries. Vero Beach, FL: The Rourke Press, Inc.

Lehn, B. (2000). What is a teacher? Brookfield, CT: The Millbrook Press, Inc.

Quiri, P. R. (1998). True book: The American flag. New York, NY: Children's Press.

Radlauer, R. S. (1992). Honor the flag. Lake Forest, IL: Forest House Publishing Company, Inc.

Schomp, V. (2000). If you were a teacher. New York, NY: Benchmark Books.

West, D. C., and West, J. M. (2000). Uncle Sam and old glory: Symbols of America. New York, NY: Atheneum Books for Young Readers.

World Book Encyclopedia (2004). Chicago, IL: World Book, Inc.

Interviews

1. Mrs. Diane Enger, *Elementary Art Teacher*
2. Mrs. Nina Maimonis, *Elementary Music Teacher*
3. Mrs. Carolyn Heiney, *Kindergarten Teacher*
4. Mrs. Margriet Ruurs, *Canadian Literary Consultant*

Steve & Debbie Layne

Steven and Deborah Layne grew up in different towns and in different states but with the same dream—to impact the future in the most dynamic way possible. Their dream came true; they became schoolteachers. Since the beginning of their marriage they have crisscrossed the grades from elementary to junior high school, falling in love with children, pouring their hearts into their work, and steadfastly believing that talented and dedicated teachers are the critical ingredient in the recipe for school success.

Steven L. Layne currently serves as Associate Professor of Education and Literature at Judson College in Elgin, Illinois. Dr. Layne is a respected literacy consultant, motivational keynote speaker, and featured author both in and outside the United States, and his writing for children and teens has been honored with multiple awards. Deborah Layne supervises preservice teachers during their clinical experiences and teaches graduate courses in literacy education. She also devotes her time to caring for her husband and children. The Laynes reside in St. Charles, Illinois.

Doris Ettlinger

Once a week Doris teaches an art class in her home and believes teaching keeps her learning. Sharing her wisdom allows Doris to reacquaint herself with art fundamentals, explore new media, and understand what young people are thinking.

Doris was born on Staten Island, New York and graduated from the Rhode Island School of Design. She now lives and works as a professional illustrator in a 150-year-old gristmill in western New Jersey with her husband, Michael McFadden, and two children, Ivy and Ben.

Doris also illustrated *G is for Garden State: A New Jersey Alphabet* published by Sleeping Bear Press in 2004. Doris's artwork can be seen at www.dorisettlinger.com